LOLA JAYE

Reaching for the Stars

HARPER

HARPER

HarperCollins*Publishers*
77–85 Fulham Palace Road,
Hammersmith, London W6 8JB

www.harpercollins.co.uk

Published by HarperCollins*Publishers* 2009
1

A catalogue record for this book
is available from the British Library

ISBN: 978 0 00 729718 4

Set in Stone Serif by Palimpsest Book Production Limited,
Grangemouth, Stirlingshire

Printed and bound in Great Britain by
Clays Ltd, St Ives plc

Mixed Sources
Product group from well-managed
forests and other controlled sources
www.fsc.org Cert no. SW-COC-1806
© 1996 Forest Stewardship Council

FSC is a non-profit international organisation established
to promote the responsible management of the world's forests.
Products carrying the FSC label are independently certified
to assure consumers that they come from forests that are managed
to meet the social, economic and ecological needs
of present and future generations.

Find out more about HarperCollins and the environment at
www.harpercollins.co.uk/green

For all those who . . . dream

Introduction

My hairbrush made a really good microphone as I pranced about in front of my full-length mirror singing 'Holiday' by Madonna. It didn't matter that I probably sounded more like a cat with a toothache because *I was going to be an international pop star!*

Of course I was!

Or South London's answer to the next big Hollywood movie star or perhaps a model instead. But not a catwalk one. I'd be one of the girls prancing about in black and white photo stories in teenage magazines. Now that's a good career, I thought, especially as it would probably come with an unlimited supply of *Jackie* magazines!

I admit it. I was a dreamer. In fact I still am. There's nothing wrong with imagining yourself on a sunny beach – as you sit on a miserable wet bench waiting for the bus. There's nothing wrong with wondering, while you stand in line at the supermarket, what it would feel like to run your own business.

There's nothing unrealistic about telling your child a story and then thinking about what it would be like to train as a teacher.

There's absolutely no reason why you shouldn't reach for a star – or two. And I hope that by reading about my journey you will begin to believe that with plenty of work, determination and a bit of dreaming, anything can be possible.

Lola Jaye, 2008

1. Dream, Dream, Dream

As I said, I'm always dreaming (even when I'm supposed to be paying attention to something else, which is most of the time). I also have a BIG imagination too. When I was little I was always thinking about what I wanted to be when I got older. I grew up with fantastic foster parents and an ever-changing number of foster children who were passing through in between other homes. So our house was always noisy with children playing. Nanny Sheila (my foster mother) would often be telling us off for jumping on chairs or fighting with each other. And there was always lots and lots of laughter.

The only problem was, the time came when I was always the oldest child in the house because I ended up staying the longest (about eighteen years!). So, as I grew up, I began to have less and less in common with the other children. And not having anyone my own age to share things with meant I was happy to stay up in my top-floor room and be by myself.

I was quite a shy person anyway, so I felt comfortable with this. Besides, writing stuff down and making up stories allowed me to create my own characters. I realized this was what I enjoyed doing most. I'd run in from school, watch a programme (or three) on TV, then get stuck into writing stories. Even so, at this time, I hadn't fully decided that I wanted to become a writer. I wanted to become the next Madonna and *then* perhaps a writer!

So what about your dreams?

You might want to manage a department store, train as a nursery nurse or even run the hurdles in the next Olympics!

There's nothing wrong with reaching for the stars because if what you catch is the moon – you haven't done too badly!

Really, Really, Really Wanting It

I suppose the first thing to think about is, 'How important is this dream to me?' Because whether or not your dream will come true can depend on how much you feel you want it. The more you want something, the more you're willing to work that bit harder for it. This can also be said for your *attitude* towards your dream or goal. If your attitude is serious enough you are more likely to be committed to making it become a reality, right?

You could say that achieving a goal is like learning to play darts. It's not the easiest thing to hit the bull's-eye. First you need to learn the right way to hold the dart, the best place to put your fingers and give a good aim at the target. It can then take time to learn the technique depending on how often you practise and how quickly you learn. But if it's something you really, really, really want, you will definitely learn faster than someone who doesn't want it that badly. You know, the person who says, 'Well, I suppose it *would* be okay to hit the bull's-eye three times in a row ... but I'm not really that bothered.' Whilst it's your dream! I know this is an odd example, but hopefully you can see what I am trying to get at.

Being Prepared

Whether you're organizing a surprise party or cooking a meal, a certain amount of planning has to go into it. For the meal, you need to make sure you have a whole lot of different things to hand, like the correct ingredients, crockery, utensils ... So something as big as

YOUR DREAM also deserves a certain amount of planning.

You need to be fully prepared if you want your dream to come true.

Putting together a list is a good way to start. It doesn't have to be a really long list, just the key things you want to achieve. So if it is your dream to open your own restaurant, your list may look a bit like this:

> Research online/books/talk to local
>   restaurant owners
> Get some practical experience in a
>   restaurant
> Look at finances and put together a
>   business plan

After I left school, I suppose you could say I was a bit greedy, because I had to have one and a half dreams. I adored writing but I also loved the idea of helping people. Training to be a doctor was out of the question because I was way too squeamish and could not bear the sight of blood. I decided instead to study to become a psychotherapist and help people who have suffered things like a breakdown or an unhappy childhood. However, I didn't have enough GCSEs to go into that field and, like many, I'd 'had it' with school. But I knew that if I wanted to help people as a psychotherapist, I needed qualifications, and that meant going on to sixth form college.

The only good thing about it was that it wasn't school. It would be in a different building, so it still felt like a great big adventure. I was excited and scared all at the same time. I was embarking on something really new. And it can feel that way for you too when you are about to face something almost unknown. This fear of the unknown: you don't know what to expect and you have no idea how things will pan out. Even at this early stage, our fears can get out of control and stop us from going any further than our lists! But don't give into this.

Don't let the fear stop you at the first hurdle.

2. Dealing With Those Negative Voices

So you've (hopefully) made a list of the key points you would like to achieve on the journey to your dream. One of the hurdles I faced when I wanted to train as a psychotherapist was the cost of paying for the course. Another was people constantly telling me I was too young.

The first hurdle I solved by applying for a career development loan, which was designed to help out with the cost of training.

The second hurdle, about my age, wasn't as easy. People around me would say things like, 'isn't she too young to train as a psychotherapist?' And, 'what does she know about life?' And, 'How can she help people?' And this was a lot harder to deal with. I was in my early twenties and I was struggling to understand how someone could judge me. How they could assume that, because of my age, I had no experience of life. They could at least have had a conversation with me first, before making that judgement.

And you may find that people around you are not as supportive as you may like. The trick is to see it as THEIR problem and not yours. Perhaps you are doing something they have always wanted to do and it bothers them that you have finally taken the plunge.

Don't allow their feelings to get in the way as you reach for those lovely stars.

Surprisingly enough, we can be very negative about ourselves. Especially if no one has ever told you that you were good at anything. Especially if the only time anyone has paid you any attention was when you were doing something wrong. Therefore, it's sometimes hard to have self-belief (which I will cover in Chapter 4). But as you inch towards your dream, watch out for this list of obstacles. They might crop up as you think about the road to following your dream:

I don't have the time
No money
I don't speak a certain way
No experience
I'm a bit 'different' to others
I'm too young
I am too old

I can't handle change
Don't have the energy
I don't have any skills
I don't know anything
I am just not good enough
I missed my opportunity years ago
It's too hard
It's too late for me to learn new things
I don't trust myself
I worry about what others will think
**It's never going to happen, so what's the
point?**

Yes, there are things we can improve on and change (like grades) but others we can't and shouldn't want to – like our race. So, if you do come across such barriers, don't allow them to pitch up a tent and live in your head – fold them away!

I have highlighted three really powerful points in the list above: 'I am just not good enough', 'I don't trust myself', and 'It's never going to happen, so what's the point?' Sometimes everything can boil down to one or more of these three statements. It usually has something to do with our past experiences. And whilst we cannot change the past, it is important not to let it rule us as we try to move forward. For example, because you have been in prison does not mean you are destined to always be in trouble with the police. You CAN change. Be confident and believe that you are the right person. Trust yourself.

You are good enough, and YOU have as much right to experience your dream as anyone else. You deserve to be happy. You don't have to settle for being unhappy, sad, depressed or anything else that takes away your power to be the person you would like to be.

Oh, and never believe those who may tell you your dream is beyond you. Just ask yourself this: *How do they know?* Think about it for just a moment. THEY DON'T KNOW! Hey, but try not to spend too much time trying to figure out why people might want to knock your confidence. Instead, use your energy to set out how you can work towards reaching for those stars and achieving your dream.

Deep down, I *knew* that I could make a good psychotherapist. I had empathy (an understanding of what other people might be going through). I knew I wanted to help people. I was also determined not to let anything like negative comments or being broke get in the way.

Nothing needs to be THAT impossible if you have the inbuilt desire to succeed in your goal. If Barack Obama can become president of the United States of America then anything is possible!

3. Dealing With Challenges

I decided to really take my childhood dream of becoming a writer seriously and try and make it a reality the day I officially became a psychotherapist. I'd been through a few personal issues and I was starting to think that life was too short and you had to try and reach for those stars as soon as you saw them. So, I sat down and thought about my hopes and dreams and what I wanted from my life. You could call this one of my Breakthrough Moments – something we will discuss in Chapter 9. And I realized I owed it to myself to begin the journey to become a writer.

So I applied the 'skills' I'd used to become a psychotherapist, again starting off with a list;

> Work
> Write in the evenings and at weekends
> Read lots
> Send off sample chapters
> Get published!

I knew it wouldn't be easy. But like before, I decided to plan for it. At the end of my planning and as I looked at my list, I realized I could work as a psychotherapist whilst I tried to become a writer in my spare time. I was finally going to go for it. After all those stories written in my top floor bedroom, I was finally going to pursue my dream of becoming a writer!

Yippee!

Okay, things are never that simple. Just saying 'I am going to do x' doesn't mean it's simply going to happen. There may be big fat challenges that crop up from time to time. Like, not being able to find the time to even make a list or being told yet again that you don't have enough experience for that job you want. If no one will give you a chance, how do you get the experience? Not having the energy to do anything other than go to bed, after a long day at work. And that good Old Faithful of emotions: Fear.

We are all faced with challenges daily, but how we deal with them is really important. In the long run, it's how we face challenges that can make us stronger. You may not believe it, but let me explain . . .

It was a challenge the day I got my very first letter from a large publisher. I had written a few chapters of my first ever novel, called Psychobabble. I sent it off and I was confident – no, I *knew* – I had written something great.

What could go wrong?

Also, I was excited that my writing was finally being seen, because as a writer, it's only you who really gets to read your work. So when I got a letter back from the publisher, I was so excited! I tore open that envelope really quickly, lots of deep breaths and started to read it. *The Managing Director of a major publishers had sent me a personal letter!* And then I read it again just to be sure I wasn't seeing things. I just couldn't believe what he had written back to me . . . Anyway, he basically said he wasn't exactly a fan of my writing, but hey, my idea was good! Oh and he wasn't interested in publishing my lovely novel, either.

What?

I was devastated.

All I wanted to do was roll under my duvet and stay there for as long as I could. Fear began to creep in again. Perhaps I was wrong to go for my dream of becoming a writer. What if I had been kidding myself? What if I just didn't have the ability?

So, as well as popping up before you've even taken the plunge, fear can also reappear once you're in the process of pursuing your dream.

Actually, it's going to pop up time and time again in the course of this book. It is such a powerful emotion. It can stop most people from taking risks and making major, potentially positive life changes. So let's look at ways you can combat it during its early stage.

First, ask yourself what you are afraid of. Jot down a list of all the things you fear will happen if you were to go for your dream.

Look at each fear individually. Ask yourself what would happen if that fear came true? Then think about how you would resolve the problem if it came about.

After that, think about all the positive things that could happen if you went for your dream, and then flip it! Start thinking about how you'd feel if you STAYED in your current situation and NEVER went for your dream. Now how does *that* feel?

For me, it was horrible to receive such a knock so early on. For a few days I almost let it make me want to give up. But I knew that I didn't want to do anything else. Writing was definitely for me. Then I unfolded the letter a few more times and began to really look at what this head honcho publishing man had said.

And my thoughts went *from*:
I'm crap at this.
I can't write. Full stop.
Give up this dream.
To:
He liked my idea but the writing was
   rubbish.
I can't write but hey, I had a good idea
   for a book.
He liked my idea!

If you look at my thought process above, you can see that I'd gone from seeing this rejection as something negative to finding a sort of positive spin to it. I was able to see that fifty per cent of the problem was solved – I had a good idea for a book. I just needed to brush up my writing skills. Of course I would have preferred it the other way round, but never mind, it was better than nothing! So, one day, I felt a surge of confidence overpower me.

If the writing wasn't good enough, then I would improve.

So I wrote and wrote, improving with each paragraph. I also bought a book on publishing, which said it was best to get an agent to work on your behalf to find a publisher. And that is what I decided to do. I was determined to

17

become a published author and nothing would stop me! The saying about 'dusting yourself off and trying again' suddenly made sense to me. I felt energized enough to carry on. I knew that without writing, I didn't know what I would do.

4. Believe in You

There may be times when it feels like no one believes in you or what you are capable of doing. So it's important that you believe in yourself at all times. I've had times when I have doubted myself. I think we all do, especially when life gets too hard. But it's a belief in your own abilities and what you are capable of that will carry you further.

Justina Ifayemi, 28, from Milton Keynes, was really passionate about getting a job after being unemployed for some time. But with a young son and having been out of the workforce for some time, she found it hard. 'I didn't want to be on the dole anymore and wanted more for me and my son. I was looking for restaurant or shop work, anything. But I suppose the employers were looking for someone with something more recent on their CV and with more experience. But if no one gives you a chance – you can't get the experience! But I wasn't going to give up. I had to believe that I could get a job.' Justina's self-belief and patience soon paid off. She joined an employment agency and got a job – her first since having her son – as a care assistant in a care home, and hasn't looked back. 'It's hard work and I have to get up at 5.30 every day. But it's giving me valuable experience in the workplace and adding to my CV. Plus, I'm really enjoying it whilst knowing it's one step towards reaching my dream which is to provide a better future for me and my son!'

As well as student debts, I had day-to-day bills to take care of. Working part time didn't help that much, but it did mean I had time to write. However, I had to make another decision as I soon realized there was just not enough money coming in. I would have to apply for full-time work – which would mean no time for writing.

When I eventually got a full-time job as a Stop Smoking counsellor, a part of me was thrilled. I had got my first paid job helping people face to face and putting my psychotherapy skills into practice. But my new fear was that I would not have enough time to write. However, my dream

of becoming a writer remained as strong as ever.
So, eventually, and with a little bit of planning,
I found a way to fit my writing around my job.
I drew up a schedule (yes, I know, another list!)
and stuck to it (most days).

Monday to Friday:
Work 9.00-5.00
6.30-7.30 dinner
8.00-9.00 write
9.00-10.00 watch TV
11.00 p.m. – bed!

Donna Douglas, 34, from London had
always dreamed of becoming a pastry chef.
She knew that just having the qualifications without any experience would make
it harder for her to find work, so she did
a spot of planning too.

'During my third year at catering college,
I got a job working in a kitchen. I had to
arrange with my employers to have two
days off a week so that I could continue
with my catering course. It meant not
having a break, but that was a sacrifice I
was willing to make to reach my dream!'

Another thing; self-belief must not be confused with arrogance.

Many of us have watched audition shows like *The X Factor* and seen some people argue with the judges when they are told that they just can't sing. Of course there are some who may go on to improve then come back. But there are also those who cannot see that perhaps singing is not for them. I sound like a cat with a toothache when I sing so, I know. But a couple of these contestants are what I like to call deluded and a bit arrogant. They truly believe they are as good as Whitney, Celine and Mariah. No amount of advice can change their minds.

So, be realistic about your dream.

What if your dream is to become a world class pianist, who travels the globe playing in massive arenas? You only started learning the other day and only practise once a week during the summer, perhaps it's best to alter it a little, to keep some of that dream alive. Perhaps you could play in a recording studio with professional singers, or just play piano as a hobby. Or if your dream is to be a world famous portrait painter but you don't know how to create paintings . . . learning to draw or simply applying for jobs in art galleries could be a way of still being around something you love.

Keep Believing

Okay, so your dream isn't to climb Mount Everest even though you are afraid of heights. It's a realistic one, therefore you must have the self-belief to see it through. You must believe that you will succeed, so that when the going gets tough – your confidence doesn't do a runner!

I enjoyed my job as a counsellor, but in the back of my mind (and the front), I knew that writing was where my heart was. There were times when I could have gone for a promotion with more money and responsibility, but I knew if I did that I'd hardly have ANY time for writing. And whilst some people thought I was mad not to try and go for a promotion, I still had that self-belief that I would one day become a writer.

To Tell or Not To Tell?

That's definitely the question. And whom you tell about your dream is a personal decision. When I'm helping people to stop smoking this is often the question I will put to them. Some say telling their loved one they are stopping smoking AGAIN, just allows others to give them a look that screams, 'Oh, what, again? Yeah right!' It's like no one believes they can do it anymore and this can be very de-motivating. Also, the constant pressure and the regular nagging ('You better not have another cigarette!') can be a little annoying.

But then, there are those who think telling others IS a good idea as they would feel that they'd be letting them down if things didn't work out and they went back to smoking. Some people feel they can use that pressure to succeed.

I did tell a small number of friends about my ambition to be a writer and most were supportive. But some found it difficult to understand. I could see it in their eyes and I couldn't blame them for that. It sounded the same as saying I wanted to become an actress or a singer, just like when I was a little girl singing 'Holiday' in front of the mirror. So I'd basically play it down as if it were a hobby, with only a few close friends really knowing how passionately I felt about writing and how far I wanted to take it.

Actress and comedienne, Jocelyn Jee Esien, did decide to tell someone about her dream:
'The only person I told was my sister (who immediately went into agent mode, bless her). I didn't shout it from the rooftops

because I knew that no one would take me seriously and I didn't want anyone to shatter my dream. Even though my dream has come true (to become a comedienne) I still dream, but bigger, as this is the engine to my passion for acting (is that corny?). Along the way, people would always tell me what my dream should be but I never listened. Now those people are my biggest fans! (How corny am I?)'

Who you tell about your dreams and goals is a really personal decision. Only you can make it, but it is an important one. Perhaps stick to those who you know will support you and take your decisions seriously.

If I'm honest, I sort of regretted telling some of the people I told. Don't get me wrong, they were supportive, it's just that I began to get fed up with the 'How's the writing going?' question, month after month and in every phone call. That was because, each time I had to tell them, 'It isn't.' And it wasn't. No agents were calling or writing back.

5. You Have To Be In It . . .

. . . To Win It

As corny as this statement is, – it's a good one, and makes a lot of sense. You see, there were a few times when I would think about what it would be like to just stop trying to reach my dream. It was feeling more and more out of reach and I was so, so tired of the knock backs.

I needed to do something. Anything.

So, for me, it was important to keep motivating myself and keep myself within the writing world. I read books by other authors, searched for websites and contacts and subscribed to writing magazines. Because if I totally took myself OUT of the writing world, then there was probably zero chance of me getting anywhere within it. This totally made sense to me.

For you, it might be an idea to look at a chance to do some work relating to your dream, even if it's unpaid. As a wannabe writer, I was writing without being paid for years! If your ambition is to be a gym instructor, taking unpaid work in, say the office of a local authority gym doesn't mean you allow yourself to be exploited. It just means you get to meet others in the business and make contacts that may be useful for you in the future. And if there's a course you want to do at the local college, grab a prospectus, apply or attend an open day. Funnily enough, Lena (one of the characters in my new book) is so afraid to apply for a course, she carries the application form around with her in her bag. This isn't a bad thing as she is still 'in' it and there is still a chance that she will send it off. The minute she chucks it away, though, there is less chance.

Carly Antoniades, 28, from London, currently follows her dream of becoming a florist whilst working at a day job:

'I'm in my fourth year of night school, training to become a florist. I also do a lot of work at weekends – at weddings and christenings – which I really love as it involves working with flowers. This way I'm already experiencing aspects of my dream, even though I still have some time to train before I reach it. Plus it's great fun!'

I meet many people who, on finding out that I am a writer, say they have always wanted to write a novel. Some have already started one, perhaps a few years ago, and it's now sitting in their bottom drawer. Others simply say they have a great idea for a book. If I ask what they have done to try and make this a reality, their reply would be, 'I have written a few pages.' There's nothing wrong with this. Perhaps they have a different dream and the urge to become a writer is not as strong as it could be.

Getting to the stage of being a writer – like most things – involves living the life that will take them to where they want to be. For example, at six o'clock on Saturday morning, when most of my friends are asleep, I'm sitting in my bed typing up my novel. That's what I do. What I'm trying to say here is, if you want success as a writer, you have to, as much as you can, live like one. And that means sending off manuscripts, getting rejection letters, and then still finding the get-up-and-go to write the fourth chapter, when someone has just rejected the first three! Snatching moments in the evening after a long day at work – even though you're really tired – because you HAVE to finish this book before your relative comes to stay next week. There can be a lot of juggling with school runs, doctor's appointments, dinner, homework, life – *whatever* your ambition.

Talk to Others Already Living Your Dream

The writers of books sitting on my shelf are not people I see every day in my street. If I did, they probably wouldn't appreciate me walking up to them and begging for advice! That's why I was so happy to have been able to send author Lisa Jewell a few samples of my first attempt at a novel many years ago. Of course, she was a busy writer and I didn't want to bother her with more requests, so I found the Internet useful during breaks in writing or when I was finding it hard to focus. Just reading about authors and searching their websites for tips and advice on how they succeeded really helped. So did finding out just how many times they got rejected before landing a publishing deal! Learning about people's experiences can be really inspiring.

After searching the Internet on yet another day, I managed to contact an editor of a large publisher. They finally agreed to look at a few chapters of my work. The result was that she liked my writing but could not persuade the rest of her team to make me an offer for the book. What I took away from that disappointing experience was the fact that a real life editor liked my writing and was willing to speak up for me. And this was a much better response than the one a few years before when that managing director had said he didn't like my writing.

I was improving.

I had to carry on.

So I continued to try and make contacts, sent out chapters to agents and wrote, wrote, wrote.

We now live in an age where there are lots of social networking sites like Facebook, Myspace and Bebo. You can become cyber 'friends' with people already living your dream, so you may find it easier to get opinions from others than I did. There are probably online forums and blogs on your chosen subject too, and again this will give you a chance to interact with others who share your dream. I started a blog a few years ago and I was able to interact with people wanting to become writers (I also used it to moan about not being published – a lot!). I also joined an online writers' forum where I was able to find out about others in the same position and some who were already published. It was all very useful, reading about those who were getting their books published and others who were in the same position as I was. Having someone you have never even met say, 'Go for it! You are very talented,' can be really uplifting.

Local libraries sometimes run or advertise some great classes too. They're not just for lending out books. Give them a try. Also, local colleges might run a course in your chosen dream. I found a creative writing class near my home, which meant I was surrounded by others sharing the same dream as me. Writing is a very solitary thing. You are mostly alone when you're tapping away, and if the person you live with is more interested in taking apart computers (as in my case), it's pretty difficult to get an opinion on your writing out of them! So spending two hours a week with a group of writers was very useful to me.

Beverly Weekes, 44, from London, is a mother of four who has recently attended a childcare course in her area. 'I hadn't sat in a classroom for over twenty-five years. So it was nerve-racking at first – sitting with all those strangers! But once I really got into it, I started to enjoy it, even though at times, I found the work a bit difficult. I recently found out I have dyslexia and this diagnosis has made me even more determined to succeed!'

I know it's not always easy to do these things, to put yourself 'out there' and network. But just letting someone know you are trying to do something is a start. They may even know someone in the same position and get you both together. A connection might be made and you will be one step closer to following your dream. Like, for example, Jayne, a young mother, who told Nicola she wanted to do a nursery nurse course but didn't know how to go about it. Nicola then told Jayne that her sister had just qualified as one and let her have her email address. Jayne then emailed Nicola's sister and found out more information about the course.

6. Stay Focused

Admittedly, focusing can sometimes be the hard part.

It's not always easy to be able to just . . . focus. There's always something else that needs doing. In my case, the washing up, or watching a certain TV programme and, oh, just having to make THAT phone call!

Understand that the only way to achieve your goals is to take action because **knowledge about something means nothing if you don't apply it.**

It can also be hard to focus when you're not feeling very motivated in the first place. For me, it would be just after a rejection letter fell through the letterbox or if I'd just had a bad day. There are lots of things that stop me from sitting down at the computer and getting on with my writing and writer's block is one such thing.

Writer's block is when my ideas just aren't in my head. I sit at the computer and nothing happens. Instead of getting too stressed out about it, I stop trying to write. I do some research online for the book or do a big spell check – anything to feel like I'm contributing to my dream (remember Chapter 5 above about being 'in it, to win it'?).

But if I really can't do anything, I watch some television, rest my mind and hope the slump doesn't last too long. At least then, I'll be refreshed for next time. **It's important to remember that you are human, NOT super-human. Chasing your dream can be really tiring! Sometimes you just need to refuel.** And this might mean just having a rest, so that when you go back to your task, your mind is clearer.

I usually try and set myself a goal of four hours of writing a day (if I am not at my day job). But I know that writing in one whole chunk of four hours would not be the best strategy. So I break the four hours down into chunks and my schedule for the day could look something like this;

Wake up
Write in PJ's for one hour
Eat breakfast
Go online (for too long)

Write for two hours
Eat lunch (whilst watching a recording of
  Desperate Housewives)
Write for another hour or more

Back to the lists again! If you are finding it difficult to focus, make a list of your goals and what you'd like to achieve and keep it safe. Then you can go back to it from time to time. You can tick things off that you have done, whilst at the same time reminding yourself of what needs doing.

If I was tempted to go to an all-night club, I'd remind myself that I was not eighteen anymore so the next day I'd probably be too tired to write. Therefore, I'd have to say no that time! I'd tell myself that although I was missing out on a potentially good night, being a writer was what I wanted to be and it was a very small sacrifice to make.

Simon Watkins, 37, from Surrey, a Global Marketing Manager for a major multi-national technology company, agrees:

'If I have an important board meeting the next day and in another part of the country, I have to make sure I am prepared, mentally and physically. So it's important that I'm as relaxed as possible the night before as I prepare my notes for the meeting. Things like a 'lads' night out' are totally out of the question. And I'm okay with that, because I like to stay focused on the end result – which is a job well done.'

You may have heard the saying, 'no pain no gain'. And although I sometimes hate this saying (who wants pain on their way to achieving something nice?), it really does make a lot of sense to me. But it can have two meanings. Firstly, that even though times are tough, discomfort is something we may go through on the way to reaching our goal. (In turn that allows us to really appreciate what we have.) Another way to look at it is that you start out knowing you'll probably have to give up something 'nice' along your journey. For example, if your dream is to lose weight, you know you will not be able to eat two chocolate bars in one sitting. Or you may have to skip a whole week of your favourite TV soap because you have homework to do for your new college course.

Sometimes things have to be sacrificed, which is why you have to keep in your mind the importance of your dream to YOU.

* * *

Chasing your dream means you have to be able to view the future you want at times. You almost have to do this in order to get through some of the challenges you may face. I'll give an example. When Martin Luther King visualized a time where his children would not be judged by the colour of their skin, he was living in a time when that was just not happening. But he had the ability to see BEYOND what he was experiencing. He was able to imagine a much, much better time. So, if you have a goal, it's important that you visualize this in your mind and as often as you need to.

In my case, for example, rejection slips from agents were arriving for me almost weekly. I was working at my day job where almost no one knew I was writing. But I still could visualize the day when I would get 'that call'.

I'm going to share something with you. It's a little exercise I used to do, not every day, but on days when I was feeling less motivated than usual. I'd imagine myself picking up a phone call from an agent who then told me my book had sold to a major publisher. Daydreaming, if you like. But it would be so vivid and so clear I could almost feel the emotions. And this let me focus more on my goal.

So why not give it a go? Visualize your dream in your head. Experience how you think you will feel when you finally grab it.

How big is your smile?

Are you excited?

Wouldn't it be great if it came true?

Visualizing how you would like your life to be is very useful. It has worked for me for many years – especially when I had to eat round at friends' houses and with family for a week because I had no food in the house. I stayed positive because I was able to visualize a time when things would improve. The hard times felt temporary because I had hope that things would get better. Just as another rejection slip didn't mean I'd never become a writer.

7. Practice Can Make Perfect

If you've been told what great photographs you take, this doesn't mean you can't learn to take even better ones. The fastest athlete at the last Olympics wasn't actually born running that fast! Doing something well needs skill and practice. Remember my darts example in Chapter 1? I suppose what I am trying to say is that your skills and abilities need to grow and get better.

For me, re-writing my manuscripts is one way to make sure I keep improving – even if at times, it can be a drag!

Professional Football Freestyler Paul (Woody) Wood, 25, knows a lot about practice. He had always wanted to be a professional footballer. But unfortunately, after spells with Wimbledon and Watford, his playing career was cut short due to injury. However, this did not deter him in his ambitions, and he was soon set to make it in the field of freestyle football. 'I train about three or four times a week, practising at my local gym for around three hours at a time. I'm surrounded by mirrors, which help me to see myself at different angles as I try out new tricks with the ball. Practice gives me the best chance to improve what I do.'

Woody is now in the hit freestyle film *In the Hands of the Gods* and able to travel the world as a professional football freestyler. All the work he has done and continues to do, has been worthwhile.

Constructive Criticism

I know. The word 'criticism' sounds really negative. But it *can* be a very positive thing if we double it up with '*constructive*'.

Constructive criticism is meant to be a good thing, a productive thing. But let's face it, the thought of any sort of criticism can be a bit scary. Who wants to hear the bad stuff? Especially when it's about something so deeply personal to you – like your dream. The trick is to take lots of deep breaths while it's being given. And don't forget to take a step back for a moment and think about what is being said to you. Hopefully, when you do this, you'll be able to sift through all the things you didn't really want to hear and perhaps think to yourself, 'This person may have a point.'

It's so important for you to understand where you may be going wrong (if at all) on your journey. Then you can take steps to improve. It's not about being treated like crap, or being negative . . . it's about being on the road to improving yourself and your skills. This can provide you with a fresh view on the dream you're working on. But:

It has to be genuine constructive criticism and the person giving it must genuinely feel so too.

So how do you go about asking for constructive criticism? Just ask someone in the 'know' which areas you could improve on or do better. Try not to ask people who are very close to you as they are more likely to say all the good stuff. And though this is nice to hear it doesn't allow you to find areas for improvement and growth. So try and find someone who is close to the subject you're seeking criticism on. If it's a website for the new business you're working on, find a web designer online and contact them with a quick email. Or your dream might be to open a bakery. In that case get a friend of a friend to sample one of your delicious creations!

Don't get me wrong, I knew I had some abilities as a writer, but I worked alone. I didn't have much feedback, so I sent my manuscript to a 'book doctor' – Hilary Johnson. She looks at manuscripts to see if they are good or need improving. After checking it over, she gave me lots of constructive criticism on my writing. Some of it was painful to read, but I knew it was necessary. At the end of it though she did say that she'd been so impressed, she'd passed it onto an agent. That was great! So, again, I chewed my poor nails nervously as I waited for the answer. I was nervous and hopeful. That chance didn't turn into a Yes for one reason or another. However, even though this was another knock back, Hilary's constructive criticisms made it a little easier to handle. I was now clear on what I needed to work on.

Review Your Strategy and Progress

If things are a little quiet, you feel, and going a bit stale on the dream front, go back to your strategies and tactics from time to time. You could start by asking yourself, just how much am I progressing? Am I getting any results, however small? Perhaps a different approach is needed. Perhaps you need to ask someone for advice. Actually this is a good place to put in the next bit: don't be afraid to ASK people for help. If you have taken my advice above, you should be in touch already with someone involved in your dream. Asking for help is not a bad thing (as long as you don't *keep* asking!).

Get on with it

As you've probably worked out, trying to get published meant being faced with a lot of setbacks. Sometimes it was another agent telling me no or yet another agent telling me . . . well, NO again. But set-backs are bound to happen along the way. It could be that two days into giving up smoking you find an old ciggie under the sofa and smoke it, or you find out the evening computer course is full after setting your heart on enrolling.

It's how you deal with each set-back that's important.

I won't say I dealt with each of my set-backs calmly. Sometimes I would clench my fists and roar out my frustration at not being able to get an agent, or I'd just mope about. But most of the time I just got on with the writing. Having said that, the hardest thing for me was letting go of the second book I'd written in order to start a new one. It was Hilary who said I should just 'get on with the next book.' And even though that was the last thing I wanted to do (again) I knew deep down that it was the only way.

So I took a deep breath and came up with yet another idea for a book, bought a new notebook, started jotting down story ideas and began to write, write and write.

I hadn't reached my dream yet, but I was still going to have a really good crack at it.

8. Mistakes Are OK Too

No, that's not a typing error.

Just the word, 'mistake', can strike fear into a lot of people's hearts. And it's the fear of making mistakes that can prevent you from chasing your dream, or reaching for a new goal, or anything that moves you out of your comfort zone.

What a total waste of your skills and talents!

First off, it's better to accept that as humans we're imperfect and basically designed to make mistakes from the moment of birth. Being human, it's probably likely you'll not only make a few mistakes in *life,* but also in what you do as you inch towards your goal. In fact you'll probably make more than a few! Just like I did when I thought it was OK to spend money I didn't have on a 'revolutionary' piece of software that would help me write my novel while I, erm . . . spoke into a mouth piece (don't ask). That was a costly mistake that not only wasted money, but also a lot of my time.

A constant fact of life is that we all make mistakes. What varies is how we each handle them. Some people get angry or upset, while others just shrug their shoulders and say; 'Mistake? Nah, that wasn't me!'

Seriously, though, how can you learn without messing up every once in a while? You need to make a mistake in order to learn. It's as simple as that.

But nobody likes making mistakes. Unless you want to go through life shut away from the world and surviving on fresh air and windy pudding, you are guaranteed to make one every now and then. But it's not all doom and gloom: **If you learn from mistakes, they can move you forward.**

Making mistakes can help us:

- Look at things differently and find new ways to fix things
- Find a solution to solve another problem we hadn't even thought of!
- Look to a newer way of thinking
- Switch directions, pace and ideas so we don't keep on doing the same wrong thing
- Learn about new things

Lots of times, they're not even mistakes! Your previous actions weren't achieving what you wanted so you went a different route that didn't turn out according to plan. That's not a mistake. We'll call it *exploration and discovery*. But if you're absolutely sure it was a mistake, then OK. But please don't spend brainpower that could be used to pursue your dream agonizing over a so-called 'mistake'. Try not to be overwhelmed with guilt and regret.

It's happened. It is in the past. So accept it (and accept that you can't change what happened). Recognize that you simply made a mistake. End of. In no way does it make you a failure because you made a mistake. You are human after all!

You and the mistake are not the same thing, so don't let it become a part of who you are.

Understand Why the Mistake Happened

Mistakes occur for various reasons. To avoid repeating them, you need to understand the reason why they came about in the first place. For example, if the mistake was to say something horrible to someone because you were angry, perhaps it's good to think about what led you to feel angry in the first place? Perhaps you were tired from cleaning out your new button shop and hadn't slept in days. If you make mistakes because you are permanently tired, try to get more rest or take time out from the task. Plus, there's no point in reaching your dream only to be too knackered to go on with it!

Avoid Repeating Mistakes

Although it's good to avoid feeling guilty about making the mistake, at the same time you should make a pact with yourself to *learn from it*. If you repeat the same mistakes, it shows you aren't making progress. It is essential to learn from the mistake so that you can move on.

Move on very quickly so that you can focus on solutions that will move you forward.

Making Mistakes In Front Of Others

Scared of showing yourself up in front of another person? Join the club. But don't worry if your mistake does happen with an audience. So what if family members know you were taken for a ride the last time you tried to make some money to fund your dream, or you ended up buying the wrong material for your T-shirt sample. It's unlikely that people really do judge us anywhere near as much as we think they do (or as much as we judge ourselves). They might actually be impressed that you are going for your dreams whilst they've sat down just 'thinking' about theirs. Plus it does seem a shame to let the fear of what someone else *might* think stop you from going further with your goal. Sometimes, we're so used to people putting us down, we almost expect it from everyone. But the truth is, you can never really know what's going on in someone else's head. You only really know what's going on in YOUR mind. And that's the thing you have control over.

If you go through life afraid to make a mistake, you'll spend most of your life doing absolutely nothing. Remember, there is no harm in making a mistake, as it can be an essential part of moving forward.

9. Breakthrough Moments

A breakthrough moment or 'Aha!' moment is a moment in time that changes everything. Perhaps that sounds a little overdramatic. I think it's different for everyone and can be huge or quite small – yet equally important. For the man whose dream it is to marry his girlfriend, getting down on one knee is a breakthrough moment. For the woman who'd always dreamed of becoming a pilot, one of her breakthrough moments would be the day she got her pilot's licence.

Of course you can have more than one breakthrough moment. But whatever they are, they have the power to move you forward and take you closer to that star you are aiming for.

Angela Buttolph is a top style journalist and expert with a high profile in magazines, television and radio. But it wasn't always like that. 'My first job was as an admin person at *ELLE* magazine, even though deep down, I really wanted to write articles. However, my breakthrough moment came one weekend when I wrote a style piece on trench coats and shyly left it on my Editor's desk on Monday morning. I wasn't sure if she'd even read it. I remember later that morning, I was in the loo, and suddenly my Editor was banging on the door shouting "get out here, this is brilliant!" – so dramatic and funny; so fashion! The feature was published in the next issue of *ELLE* magazine; October 1994! And I've been writing articles (and a lot more!) ever since!'

One of my breakthrough moments was taking the first three chapters of my new novel to the Winchester Writers' Conference. An X Factor for writers, if you like, that brought writers, agents and publishers together under one roof. Having already sent in some chapters to two agents, I was looking forward to meeting them and getting their opinion on my work. This was my new novel and no one except me had seen it before. Yikes! I couldn't stop smiling the entire time I was there as I mingled with other people who shared my dream. The first agent I had an appointment with did not seem interested in me at all. The second agent, Simon, was friendly, chatty and positive enough about the book. But he wanted to see more chapters before making a decision about taking me on. Now I had to clean out my ears to make sure I had heard him correctly. *Was he really considering taking me on?* I couldn't breathe. This was THE most exciting news ever. I had to stay calm because I still had another agent to see, one who had rejected my earlier manuscript a few years back.

The agent, Judith, didn't look that excited as I sat before her and started discussing my story.

Minutes felt like hours and she finally looked up.

'I like it, but . . .'

'But?' I asked.

'It needs reworking . . .'

Again, I held my breath and my smile, wanting to scream, 'YES!' to everyone and anyone. Two agents had asked me to send them the remaining chapters of my book! Of course I had been here before . . . so close, but this felt different, it had to be. Only problem was – I still had to write the rest of the novel!

And that was one of my breakthrough moments.

Grabbing that Opportunity

As I said, you can have more than one break-through moment. But what you do with that opportunity is just as important, if not more so. For example, you're wearing one of your own fashionable creations as you walk up the high street when you are stopped by a well-known television presenter and asked, 'Where can I get that lovely T-shirt?' I hope you'll be bold enough to give her a phone number or email – even if you've only made a few that you gave away to family and friends. After all, it's about seizing opportunities. But I know this can be hard. Again, fear and our own insecurities can get in the way as old questions reappear: 'Am I good enough?' 'Can I do this?' Well, if you've got that far, then a few more miles won't hurt.

Of course, breakthrough moments aren't always things that land in your lap... sometimes you have to put yourself in the position to be able to receive one. Like I did by booking myself into a place where I knew there'd be lots of publishing people about – therefore it didn't 'just happen'. Likewise, if your dream is to work full time for a charity, putting yourself forward for voluntary work a couple of hours a week will put you in a better position to get full time paid work.

Each breakthrough moment will keep moving you forward and closer to that star.

Hopefully, you will have a few breakthrough moments, but when and how you get to the next one depends on how you treat the current one. I spent the days following my breakthrough moment working furiously on the new novel. I had about twenty-five more chapters to write! I took some time off work and said a temporary goodbye to a social life. I finally put the full stop on the last sentence of my 80,000-word novel a few months later. I sent it to both agents and waited.

The first reply finally arrived in the post. It was from Simon, who said a nice enough No. But this was followed by Judith's whopping great big fat YES!!!!!!!!!!!!!!

I finally had an agent.

10. Don't forget to live your life!

It felt absolutely fantastic to finally get an agent.

My daydreams and visualizations were finally coming true. I hoped it would only be a matter of time before a publisher was interested. We worked on getting the manuscript just right for publishers to have a look at. But when they did, I didn't get the response I had hoped for.

I was *still* getting rejected. The only difference was that the bad news came through my agent. I was getting closer to my dream, almost touching it, but not close enough. Again, I was advised to get on with the *next* book, and I followed it. But this time I decided to write in a different style. I'm not sure why I did this. Perhaps I wanted to try something different, or perhaps because of the set-backs my confidence and self-belief were doing a runner on me!

Patience is Necessary

As I was finding out, a dream can take some time to truly blossom. But there are some people who look like they achieved their dreams overnight. I always like the term 'overnight sensation' when it's used to describe a new singer. What we're not told about are the years of singing in dingy bars, perhaps being booed off stage and having to tour in a clapped-out camper van! People who achieve greatness don't usually do it overnight. So don't think it's going to happen overnight. There'll be times when absolutely nothing seems to be working. But the trick is to celebrate any small successes you have on the journey to your dream.

Reaching Round and Patting yourself on the Back

I celebrated every time I finished a draft of my manuscript or thought of a new story idea, even when I didn't have an agent or publisher. It was something I did for ME. I'd cook a special meal or go out with friends as a treat. It was an acknowledgement of achieving something, however small. When you achieve one of your goals, celebrating it can really help to build your self-confidence. This way, each goal you reach will boost you up and help you set even bigger goals for your future. For example, if it's your goal to lose a stone in weight, each pound lost deserves a pat on the back. If your goal is to stop smoking, every day without a cigarette should be celebrated. Perhaps you can use the money that you would have spent on one pack of cigarettes to buy yourself a little treat. And then allow yourself to think about the next goal.

It's important that YOU rely on yourself to do the 'patting', as people around us can change. Although they might be lovely and supportive in the beginning, they may get bored with all the 'well dones'. They may simply begin to think you don't need their encouragement any more. And this is where YOU come into it. Keep motivating and re-motivating yourself regularly. If you have managed to learn a whole sentence in your Spanish class without looking at the textbook, tell yourself 'well done!' **These are small steps, yes, but steps that are taking you closer and closer to your dreams.**

Take a Break

For me, having to start all over again AGAIN was starting to make me feel tired, physically and emotionally. It also added to the lack of self-belief it brought on. If this happens to you, you may find the following useful:

That old thing called visualization again. But this time, use it to help you with something OUTSIDE of your dream.

- Think about times when you have felt happy, good or content. Who were you with? Where were you? What were you up to?
- Make more time in your life for what is important to you.
- Focus on what's positive instead of the negative. You could even write down a few positive things about yourself. This isn't an easy exercise (although when asked to put down negative points, it usually is!).
- Think of ways you got through unhappier times in the past. This could have been staying with a good mate for a long weekend; going for long walks;

praying; seeking advice from a loved one.

- If the pursuit of your dream isn't going to plan, maybe you have fantastic health? A loving partner? Great kids? A roof over your head? Look at what's going WELL in your life right now and focus on that.

I managed to work through my low patch and slowly began to feel happy again. Even though I still hadn't got a publishing deal, I realized my whole life wasn't about writing. I saw the importance of embracing life NOW. I'd been turning down invitations so that I could write. I wasn't seeing much of the world around me. I'd become so strict with myself that I'd lost perspective and this wasn't good for me or my writing.

Yes, you have to make sacrifices to follow your dream, but you need to strike that balance. There will be times when you will be busier than usual, especially if you are at a crucial stage of achieving your goal. For me, it's at the beginning and end of a draft.

But you shouldn't be focused on your goal ALL the time.

Take a break from pursuing your dream from time to time. I'm sure we all know people who seem to live by the 'all work and no play' line. Remember, we only get one chance on this earth and working all the hours doesn't seem like a balanced use of the time we do have. It's important to take time out to enjoy the simple things in life, like the sunshine, spending time with family and friends, sleeping. A balanced lifestyle should lead to a balanced mind and a better outcome in whatever your goal happens to be.

Tomorrow isn't promised so let's live well, today.

11. One 'No' Too Many

I admit it. The knock backs were getting me all in a tiz.

It's never a good thing to keep hearing 'No' over and over. If we look back at a lot of my journey, it was something I heard a lot.

But what about when it just gets too much?

Especially when it happens so often you are almost used to it and, at times, expect it. So, if the bank manager says no to the small business loan, or the college rejects your application, or you fail yet another driving test, or if another agency refuses to take you on because of your criminal record . . . what then? It's sometimes so easy to tell yourself, 'I knew it would happen anyway.'

When we are used to knock backs, we soon start to expect them.

Joanne Collins, 33, from London, is a Child and Adolescent Clinical Psychology Specialist. She says:

'The young people I work with struggle

to change because it is difficult finding work and getting the money they need to support themselves (or their children). The temptation of the street is strong as they feel they have no other options. I often tell them that it's about doing what's right for them, whilst remembering that there is a better way. They also need to have faith in their abilities. And at the time when they are serious about change they need to recognize negative voices in their life and shut them down!'

It is so important to tell yourself that you deserve to be happy. You deserve to achieve your dream – as long as you are willing to put the work in.

Staying True to Yourself

My new book in a new style was almost finished and I gave it to my agent to read. She phoned and simply said 'Lola, you have lost your voice.' Meaning it just didn't sound like 'me'. It's then I switched off my ears in defiance, but not before hearing her say something that has stayed with me. It was sometimes I see as another of my Breakthrough Moments:

'Is this the novel you have always wanted to write, Lola?'

No. It wasn't.

I put down the phone feeling angry. I had taken a risk with a new style of writing and it hadn't paid off. I continued with my blog called Diary of an Unpublished Author, realizing I remained just that – unpublished.

But one day I woke up feeling so low, I was just so FED UP. I'd worked so hard and yet nothing was happening. What more could I do? Of course I'd had feelings like that before, but the difference is I was bored with them. I hung around at home dressed in my pyjamas and switched the television on. Oprah Winfrey was doing a show about a dying mother who left a collection of keepsakes for her daughter. A couple of 'what if' questions flooded into my head.

- What if there were no computers, DVDs, MP3s, video cameras or phones?
- What about a dad who died and simply left a letter to his daughter?
- What if I switch on my computer and see what happens?

I did . . . and I wrote six thousand words that day.

The words flowed out of me like a waterfall.

The feeling was so satisfying and so real, I just knew I was onto something. Okay, I confess, I always feel that way when I write a new novel, but I like to think there was an extra sprinkling of magic that day, considering all that had happened so far.

And so my novel, *By The Time You Read This . . .* was born.

I had stayed true to myself and written a novel I was proud of. I had written as ME. I wasn't trying a different style of writing, I wasn't trying to be like anyone else– I was staying true to myself, Lola Jaye. I am not saying that change can't be a good thing because it can. Just make sure that, in the meantime, you do not compromise who you are as a person. That passage is a bit deep I know and will mean different things for different people depending on the stars they are trying to reach.

And then the strangest thing happened. My agent phoned and told me a publisher was interested in my novel and wanted to meet me.

A publisher finally wanted to meet me.

HarperCollins wanted to meet me.

Number one on my list of publishers I used to daydream about.

You'd think, with all the knock backs, I'd be jumping for joy and shouting from the rooftops, right? Wrong. Instead, I felt really cautious. I kept telling myself it didn't mean they wanted to *publish* me, it was just a meeting. By doing this I was letting all the previous knock backs get to me, again.

It's sometimes hard to allow yourself to believe that something good is happening to you.

Some people even think they don't DESERVE to have good things happen to them. For example, if someone has had a hard time growing up, it can be very difficult for them to accept that good things are finally happening. Or if you have always been told you would never achieve anything, it can be hard to accept that you HAVE achieved something good.

I remember feeling a little excited as I walked up to the huge HarperCollins building. I felt a little nervous and a little happy – but I didn't let it show. Although I had never got this far before, I was used to getting rejections. A part of me was protecting myself against another one.

Luckily, the meeting went great. I met with my agent, an editor and the head of publicity at HarperCollins. The building I had daydreamed about was actually real. With bricks, a floor and everything! The people were also real, not images in my imagination. This wasn't a visualization. This wasn't a daydream.

This was real.

A day later, they, HarperCollins made an offer for my book.

When Judith, my agent, told me about the offer, I felt . . . nothing. I'm not sure why. Perhaps it was because after all those years, I felt drained of any emotion. I suppose I felt numb. It wasn't until three hours after the phone call that I dared to say to myself, 'I'm a writer. I am a writer!' I still had a fear, deep down, that things could even now go 'belly up'. That the publishers could have a change of heart. When I told a few mates and a few colleagues at work, I had one eye on the phone. I hoped there wouldn't be a call telling me that the publishers had made a mistake and they had decided not to publish my book after all.

You may find that this happens a lot when you experience moments that bring you closer to your dream. However small or big the joy you receive, make sure you allow yourself to experience it. You deserve it and you have worked hard for it – I just needed to follow that advice, too!

Friends and colleagues continued to tell me I was too calm. But one night I got home from work and my neighbour said; 'I have something for you.' It was a bunch of flowers (delivered while I was at work) from my publishers. How my heart raced that evening as I danced around my flat, singing, giddy, happy and finally enjoying *my moment!!*

At last.

12. Reaching That Star

What followed was a whirlwind.

The publishers gave a champagne reception for me where I met lots of people. I was greeted with, 'I really enjoyed your book, Lola!' Now that was weird. For months the characters in my book *By The Time You Read This*... had been living in my head. Now people I had never met before were telling me how much they had enjoyed reading about them! The whole experience was amazing. I was closer and closer to realizing my dream of having a published book in the shops. I allowed myself to experience the joy and the happiness, while at the back of my mind wondering if it was acceptable to feel this H.A.P.P.Y.

I know I've mentioned it before but I have to say it again: fear can prevent us from doing so much with our lives. Even if you get over the fear of applying for a job you have wanted for ages and send off the application form, the fear starts all over again if you get an interview.

'Will they like me?' Then if you get the job it's, 'Will I be able to fit in?' Then it's, 'Will I be able to get that promotion?' Mine was, 'What if it all goes wrong and then I get to look like a wally?'

How you react to finally reaching your goal, whether it is passing a test, winning a football match, or being offered a job you never thought you'd get, is personal to you. You may scream out from the top of your voice or dance around the street in a silly hat. Just make sure you mark it in some way and don't let fear take over.

From a Dream to Reality

Even though my dream was fast becoming a reality, I was still not able to take my own advice and allow myself to enjoy the moments that kept coming my way. On top of the disbelief I have talked about above, I suppose I also didn't want people around me to think I had suddenly got big headed. Who knows? All I know is, when my publishers organized a photo shoot for my book jacket, I forgot all about my insecurities and really went for it. It was a cold December morning and me and the professional photographer, Joby, did some shots of me in and outside my home. Being photographed by a professional and knowing it was for the cover of my book made it all the more exciting. I remember one text that came through on my phone that day as I pranced about pretending to be an ageing supermodel. It said:

'Enjoy it. You deserve it.'

The same goes for you and whatever your dream happens to be – *you deserve it*. Keep reminding yourself of this. I know there is a fine line between arrogance and confidence. But try and keep confident even when it's the last thing you feel. Motivate, re-motivate and then motivate again.

Almost There

When the time came for me to see my real book being published, my editor Claire kindly arranged for me to watch it being printed. My book multiplied time and time again and spat out of huge machines; oh the noise, the joy, the excitement. I can't even describe how it really felt (I know, and I'm supposed to be a writer!). All I can say is that it was absolutely amazing and was ONE OF THE BEST DAYS OF MY LIFE SO FAR. It was hard not to jump about like a mad woman, screaming and shouting, so I did!

I wasn't holding back anymore I WAS FULLY ENJOYING MY MOMENT! I just couldn't believe that my book was actually being printed in front of me. Wow. I felt like that little girl again singing in front of the mirror with my hairbrush.

When my book was actually handed to me, all gleaming, fresh and new, I didn't dare open it. I just kept staring at it in wonder, with this really gormless expression on my face. In my hands was my newly published book, a real book. The same book that would be sold in bookshops and supermarkets across the United Kingdom, Australia, New Zealand and parts of Canada!

My book!

Unleashing *Your* Dream

It's here.
You're smelling it.
You're tasting it.
You're living it.
Your dream.
There are many ways that you can keep your position once you have reached your dream. A

comedian who finally reaches his dream of playing at the Royal Variety Performance can avoid becoming too complacent or 'comfortable' by constantly working hard to keep putting out great jokes. Similarly, I will continue to write and try to get better at it.

In the meantime, I had a launch party to go to.

Mine.

With days to go before the official publication of my book *By The Time You Read This . . .* I threw a launch party for my family, friends and colleagues. This was my way of presenting my book to my world. But it was also my way of saying; 'Look, I've done it!'

Of course a prickle of fear appeared. This time it was, 'What if no one turns up?' But I need not have worried, because when I walked into the bar in Piccadilly Circus I found myself faced with a hundred or so people waiting for me! Almost everyone I had invited had turned up and I seriously couldn't believe it at first, especially when they started to cheer and clap. It was then that I started jumping about screaming, madly excited at everything. Personally, I think I was screaming for the last few stressful days, months, years it had taken for me to get to where I was – oh, and the shock of seeing that almost everyone had shown up!

Speeches followed, and my editor Claire mentioned just how enthusiastic and hard-working I was. Even though this produced lighthearted scoffs from a few former work colleagues, I was so grateful that she recognized these points in me. It has and will always be important to me for people to know that things were not handed to me on a plate. **Getting published, like most dreams, is something that took hard work, determination and drive.**

I began my speech with; **'Success is 1% inspiration and 99% perspiration . . .'**

I thanked a whole bunch of people I felt had played a part in my getting to where I was. Hilary was there, and I let her know that her support over the years had never been forgotten. I still have to find the editor who tried to 'push' me at her publishers, but find her I will, if only to thank her for her belief in me all those years ago. Because no matter how hard you work, if there are people along the way who have tried for you, or even said a few kind and encour-aging words, it's always good to find them when you have reached your star. Let them know how their contribution was appreciated.

That evening I signed my freshly published books, feeling more and more like a writer as the night went on. It was strange to think that people would soon be peering deep into my private thoughts and seeing pieces of my imagination through the pages of my book. I'd been so private with my writing in the past – and now almost everyone I knew was about to start reading my work, MY DREAM! What an amazing and scary thought!

Indeed, depending on what your goal is, when you reach it, it then becomes more than just 'your thing'. It becomes something to some-body else too. An example would be your skill as a gym instructor: once you have qualified and you have clients, they are then using your skill to try to become fitter. When you finish your training as a caterer, the dishes you make will be eaten by others. In both these exam-ples, your dream has become something to someone else, and this means it's going to be judged. That sounds heavy. But I dealt with those feelings on the night of my launch party as I noticed people flicking through the pages of my book, ready to read them as soon as they could. I was tempted to say, 'Be nice. It's fragile. It (or I) has feelings . . .' But I didn't, because, actually, my book is strong, it's robust and so am I. It's the book I have always wanted to write. It can look after itself now (and besides, I had Book Two needing my attention!). So that night I let my book go off into the world to be judged and looked at. And I was fine with that. You will be too, as long as you are confident that you have given it your all and very best. Self-belief, confidence in your abilities and/or the product you are trying to get off the ground, remains utterly important, because if you don't have it – who else will?

13. The Sky's The Limit

The morning after my book launch, I checked out of the hotel I'd booked myself into as a launch treat. I just happened to bump into a certain Mr Will Smith – yes the actor – as he was leaving a press conference for Nelson Mandela's birthday celebrations. And this was BIG on so many levels. Not least because I had mentioned him in my speech the night before AND had always imagined Will Smith as my main character in *By The Time You Read This* . . . (that's if it is ever made into a movie!). But to say the least, it was timely and an absolute joy to see him the day after the launch party and the day the book had started to appear in the shops.

It was one of those moments. It was a moment I knew was unlikely to happen again, so I had to strike, quickly, knowing I had just a few seconds. As the photographers ignored me and took lots of pictures of Mr Smith, I called out to him, and he called me over. As we hugged, I quickly told him I had written a book with him in the lead role and that I wanted him to play it!!!!!! I gave him my card, which he took very graciously before joining his lovely wife Jada in the car. I was shaking when I did this, but I did it nevertheless.

Hey, it's my DREAM after all!

Once I had calmed down it was time to take a look in the shop and see my books on display for the very first time.

There they were, sitting on a shelf. My dream. Little stars shining for all to see.

By The Time You Read This . . . by Lola Jaye.

Wow.

And then I had to take a moment to think about all those years of struggle, hope, lack of hope, prayer, determination, disappointment, visualization, sweat, daydreaming, happiness, fears and tears, realizing it had all come down to this wonderful and beautifully special point in time.

Never Stop Dreaming

When I was fourteen, I remember really wanting a particular pair of Adidas trainers. My best friend Donna wanted a pair of British Knights. Both cost over seventy pounds. With one pound a week pocket money, I was going to have to save for the rest of my life, and by then the trainers wouldn't be in fashion any more! I knew there was no point in even asking my foster mum for the money, as things were very tight. So my friend and I both decided to get a job. The trainers were our goal and we were determined to buy the ones we wanted.

After lots of CVs handed in at various shops, we finally got jobs with a football pools organization. It got us out of bed on a Saturday morning. That bit was hard, but what kept us going was the thought of our brand spanking new trainers. The day came soon enough, when we were able to afford them I will never forget how it felt to open up that box of fresh-smelling trainers.

On top of this, my friend and I stayed at our jobs because we liked the independence of having our own money and the confidence a job gave us. We felt like real grown-ups, and, another plus, we made new friends too. I remember our tea breaks were spent around a large table in the dining room with other teenagers. Donna would bring in freshly made sandwiches that tasted like no other, while a very funny girl we made friends with lit up our tea breaks with her energy and madcap jokes. We never spoke a lot about what we wanted to be when we grew up, but ambitions were mentioned from time to time. It wasn't hard to see what interested these two girls: Donna is now a successful pastry chef, and Jocelyn is a comedienne with her own show on BBC2!

I suppose the point I am trying to put across here is: I once dreamt of a fresh-smelling pair of trainers, and also dreamed of becoming a writer. They are not on the same level, but they are dreams nevertheless. I am constantly dreaming. And you could be too.

As you know, I had been dreaming about the moment I would become a published author for a very, very long time. And now it's here, does this mean I've stopped dreaming? Before I answer that question, I want to raise something here about having a dream, a goal, a vision of where you want to get to. It is such an important starting point.

During my first event as an author, I was invited to a library to meet some school children. The first lot of children were very young – around eleven or twelve years old. They were lively and enthusiastic and I answered a lot of their questions. I also wanted to get across the point that they could be anything they wanted to be as long as they had the determination and were willing to put in the hard graft. They seemed OK with that suggestion.

When the older kids arrived (aged about fifteen) I knew the group would be a different experience and a lot harder. They weren't going to give me an easy ride – but hey, they are teenagers, and we were all like that once... But I suppose the contrast with the earlier group shocked me, because I wasn't prepared for the blankness I got back when I asked the question, 'What is your dream?' A few shrugged shoulders, and finally one boy said, 'I don't have one,' and this made me sad. At his age, not all of my friends knew what they wanted to be, but most had dreams and some sort of plan for how to get there. Or they had at least thought about *something,* whether it was working with animals, or being an astronaut, or a baker...

After a bit of prodding, the boy with no dream mentioned that he liked football and enjoyed music. It was a start, I thought. But his lack of enthusiasm saddened me still. Or perhaps he was just a shy child and his dreams were tucked away in his mind to remain private. I'd like to think so. After that, at the library, it was nice when a young girl came up to me and asked me to sign my book for her. Then without warning she said, 'Do you think I can do it?' I wondered what she meant. I could hardly hear her as she spoke so softly. 'Do you think I can become a lawyer?' she said. I looked at her and said, 'You can do anything you want to. Who told you you couldn't become a lawyer?'

'Everyone.'

I was very grateful to have spoken to that girl because it gave me hope that some young people are still dreaming. And that is pleasing.

As for me, no, I'll NEVER stop dreaming.

A Little More Hard Work...

I'm now a published author, so all I have to do is sit back and enjoy it... Wrong! I have another book to finish writing (which incidentally is called – *While You Were Dreaming*...). And then it's back to meetings, edits, re-writes, covers. Juggling the day job, life. But I don't mind because this is the type of work I really, really enjoy.

Remember what I said about enjoying your dream? That is so important. I'm not saying your goal will always feel like fun. There will be times when you are just not in the mood, you are tired or your brain just won't function the way you want it to. But for the most part, it should be satisfying, rewarding and something you can see yourself doing for a long time.

I'm told we live in a celebrity age, where people want to get on a reality television show and earn lots of money, or date a famous celebrity and, again, get lots of money – quickly. I'm not going to judge anyone. I'll simply say that, when you have worked hard for something over a period of time, it feels all the more lovely to finally have it in your grasp. Like wearing my lovely trainers felt all those years ago. Like becoming a published author feels today.

The challenges don't stop just because you have reached for that star and caught it! New challenges just appear in place of the old ones. If the challenge before was finding the time to pursue your dream, the time issue might even have got worse. For me, juggling the day job with the writing became even more difficult. When I dropped a day at work, things got a little better.

Other challenges can arise once you are touching your dream, like dealing with people's jealous reactions to your achievements, or people thinking you are suddenly richer than the queen, or not coping well with the sudden increase in responsibility and work. Many challenges may arise, but when they do, just face them like you did the earlier ones. The strength you used when reaching for your dream will be the same type of strength needed to combat new challenges and deal with the rewards that will come your way once you are achieving your goal.

Now, as a newly published author, nothing and EVERYTHING has changed.

My book, *By The Time You Read This* . . . has sold to other countries and will be translated into many other languages.

As I start on this new journey as a writer, living the dream I first visualized as a little girl, here are a few last points I'd like to share with you:

- Never forget where you came from
- Don't look for your dream to make you happy
- You are responsible for your own actions and how you respond to things.
- Balance your goals with everything else in your life

- Keep those that you love and trust close to you: they'll be the ones who encourage and support you through good and bad times
- Never, never, never give up trying to reach your dream
- Reach for those stars, grab hold of them, feel, enjoy, and never let them go!

Acknowledgments and Further Resources

Oodles of thanks to my case study contributors!

Angela Buttolph – www.angelabuttolph.com

Paul (Woody) Wood –
  www.paulwoodfreestyle.com

Jocelyn Jee Esien

Justina Ifayemi

Donna Douglas

Carly Antoniades

Joanne Collins

Beverly Weekes

Simon Watkins

Courses and Funding

www.learndirect.co.uk
Telephone: 0800 101 901
www.connexions-direct.com
Telephone: 080 800 13 2 19

www.princes-trust.org.uk
Telephone: 0800 842 842
www.direct.gov.uk
www.hotcourses.com
www.floodlight.co.uk

Quitting Smoking

www.quit.org.uk
Telephone: 0800 00 2200
www.nhs.uk/gosmokefree
Telephone: 0800 169 0 169

Healthy Eating

www.bhf.org.uk
Telephone: 08450 708070
www.bda.uk.com

Bits & Bobs for other budding Writers!

www.authonomy.com
www.writersconference.co.uk
www.hilaryjohnson.demon.co.uk

Quick Reads

Books in the Quick Reads series

Quick Reads

Pick up a book today

Quick Reads are bite-sized books by bestselling writers and well-known personalities for people who want a short, fast-paced read. They are designed to be read and enjoyed by avid readers and by people who never had or who have lost the reading habit.

Quick Reads are published alongside and in partnership with BBC RaW.

We would like to thank all our partners in the Quick Reads project for their help and support:

Arts Council England
The Department for Innovation, Universities and Skills
NIACE
unionlearn
National Book Tokens
The Vital Link
The Reading Agency
National Literacy Trust
Welsh Books Council
Basic Skills Cymru, Welsh Assembly Government
Wales Accent Press
The Big Plus Scotland
DELNI
NALA

Quick Reads would also like to thank the Department for Innovation, Universities and Skills; Arts Council England and World Book Day for their sponsorship and NIACE for their outreach work.

Quick Reads is a World Book Day initiative.
www.quickreads.org.uk   www.worldbookday.com

Quick Reads

The Dare
John Boyne

Black Swan

At the start of his school holidays, Danny Delaney is looking forward to a trouble-free summer. But he knows that something terrible has happened when his mother returns home one afternoon with two policemen.

There has been an accident. Mrs Delaney has hit a small boy with her car. The boy is in a coma at the local hospital and nobody knows if he will ever wake up.

Danny's mother closes herself off, full of guilt. Danny and his father are left to pick up the pieces of their broken family.

John Boyne tells the story from the point of view of a twelve-year-old boy. *The Dare* is about how one moment can change a family forever.

Other resources

Free courses are available for anyone who wants to develop their skills. You can attend the courses in your local area. If you'd like to find out more, phone 0800 66 0800.

 Don't get by get on 0800 66 0800

A list of books for new readers can be found on www.firstchoicebooks.org.uk or at your local library.

 The Vital Link

Publishers Barrington Stoke (www.barringtonstoke.co.uk), New Island (www.newisland.ie) and Sandstone Press (www.sandstonepress.com) also provide books for new readers.

Barrington Stoke   OPEN DOOR   SANDSTONEPRESS
CONTEMPORARY QUALITY READING

The BBC runs a reading and writing campaign. See www.bbc.co.uk/raw.

RaW
BBC

www.quickreads.org.uk   www.worldbookday.com